D1162264

CELEBRITY SECRETS

SOCCER STARS

ADAM SUTHERLAND

PowerKiDS
press

New York

Published in 2012 by The Rosen Publishing Group, Inc.
29 East 21st Street, New York, NY 10010

First Edition

Senior Editor: Camilla Lloyd
Designer: Stephen Prosser

Picture Acknowledgments: The author and publisher would like to thank the following for allowing their pictures to be reproduced in this publication: Cover and 6: Jewel Samad/AFP/Getty Images; © Luke MacGregor/Reuters/Corbis: 8; AFP/Getty Images: 18; Bongarts/Getty Images: 22 (bottom); Chelsea FA/Getty Images: 23 (bottom); Rex Features: 5, 9, 12, 13, 14, 16, 19, 20, 21, 22 (middle); photoplanet.am/Shutterstock: 1, 7; sportgraphic/Shutterstock: 2, 10, 11, 22 (top), 23 (middle); afaizal/Shutterstock: 4; Jonathan Larsen/Shutterstock: 15, 23; Brandon_Parry/Shutterstock: 17.

Library of Congress Cataloging-in-Publication Data

Sutherland, Adam.
 Soccer stars / by Adam Sutherland. — 1st ed
     p. cm. — (Celebrity secrets)
 Includes index.
 ISBN 978-1-4488-7038-7 (library binding) — ISBN 978-1-4488-7086-8 (pbk.)
 — ISBN 978-1-4488-7087-5 (6-pack)
 1. Soccer players—Biography—Juvenile literature. I. Title.
 GV942.7.A1S87 2012
 796.334092'2—dc23
 [B]

                                        2011029066

Manufactured in Malaysia

CPSIA Compliance Information: Batch #WW2102PK: For Further Information contact Rosen Publishing, New York, New York at 1-800-237-9932

Contents

Wayne Rooney

ENGLISH HITMAN

Rooney is an energetic player on the field. He runs around 7.5 miles (12 km) each game!

Stats!

Name: Wayne Mark Rooney

Date of birth: October 24, 1985

Clubs: Everton (2002–2004), Manchester United (2004–present)

Position: Striker

First break: Rooney joined Everton when he was still in school and rose through the ranks. Five days before his 17th birthday, he made his professional debut against Arsenal. He scored the winning goal, ending Arsenal's 30-match unbeaten run, and became the youngest goal scorer in England's Premier League history.

Major achievements: With Manchester United Rooney has won the Premier League three times (2006–2007, 2007–2008, 2008–2009) and the Champions League in 2008. He has also won the Professional Footballers Association (PFA) Young Player of the Year award twice (2004–2005 and 2005–2006) and the PFA and Football Writers' Player of the Year awards in 2009–2010. The awards have the word football in their names because that is what soccer is called in most parts of the world.

Secrets of success: Rooney is one of England's most naturally gifted players and a great goal scorer. He is also a hard worker who always gives 100 percent and can't stand losing!

As a kid, Rooney played for Everton Under-9s against Manchester United and scored six goals, including a perfect overhead kick!

Life Story

Wayne Rooney burst onto the Premier League scene as a 16 year old in 2002 with a wonder goal against Arsenal and has not looked back since. After two years with his hometown club, Everton, he joined Manchester United in August 2004. Since then he has won just about every trophy in English soccer.

As the first choice striker for his team and for the England team, Rooney has to shoulder the responsibility for his team's success. At times, including the 2010 World Cup in South Africa, it can be a lot to handle, but mostly he rises to the challenge and plays with the infectious energy and enthusiasm of a kid, running up and down the field and challenging for every ball.

Rooney plays with Manchester United in the Premier League in August 2010 at a stadium called Old Trafford.

Questions and Answers

Q You seem to work very hard on the field, helping your defenders as well as trying to score goals.

A "You know, I do that because I want to win. I should probably save my energy and stay up front, but I think it's just the way I have been brought up. I want to win and I try to give everything to do that."

Wayne Rooney, The Mirror, *February 2010*

Q As a striker, you often get the credit when your team wins. Is that fair?

A "No. [Soccer] is a team game and it's the whole team that should take credit, not just individual players. Every member of the squad plays their part and as a team we win together and we lose together."

Wayne Rooney, fourfourtwo.com, 2009

When his strike partner Cristiano Ronaldo left Manchester United for Real Madrid, fans were worried they would miss Ronaldo's goals. Instead, Rooney stepped into Cristiano Ronaldo's shoes and enjoyed his greatest goal-scoring season with 34 goals, 26 in the Premier League. Rooney never ever wants to be beaten!

Cristiano Ronaldo

MATCH WINNER

Ronaldo celebrates after scoring in the World Cup in Cape Town, South Africa in 2010.

At Manchester United, Ronaldo stayed behind at training for 30 minutes every day just practicing free kicks.

Stats!

Name: Cristiano Ronaldo dos Santos Aveiro

Date of birth: February 5, 1985

Clubs: Sporting Lisbon in Portugal (2001–2003), Manchester United (2003–2009), Real Madrid in Spain (2009–present)

Position: Winger, also called wide midfielder

First break: Ronaldo joined his local team Andorinha, in Portugal when he was eight. Two years later he signed with C. D. Nacional and, after helping them win the youth league, he was offered a trial with Sporting Lisbon. He joined Lisbon's academy and was the only player to play for Under-16s, Under-17s, Under-18s, the B-team, and the first team all in the same season!

Major achievements: Won the Premier League three times with Manchester United (2006–2007, 2007–2008, 2008–2009), the Football Association Challenge Cup, or FA Cup, in 2004 and the Champions League in 2008. He was named European Player of the Year in 2007 and World Player of the Year in 2008.

Secrets of success: Ronaldo is a master of the dribble—fast, with great close ball control. His free kicks are also legendary. According to experts, he is able to generate speed and dip on the ball by shifting his bodyweight forward and slicing his foot across the ball on impact.

Life Story

When Ronaldo moved to Manchester as an 18 year old from his home in Madeira, Portugal, he was so homesick he used to cry every time he spoke to his family on the telephone. Now the world's most expensive soccer player, who joined Real Madrid in the summer of 2009, remembers those times as helping him develop the necessary mental toughness to succeed in his chosen profession.

Questions and Answers

Q When did you start playing soccer?

A "I started to play in Madeira in the street. The kids there still love to play [soccer]. From an early age my dream was to become a professional [soccer player], I did it and now I can say, never give up. Opportunities come to [everyone], we must know how to grasp them."

Cristiano Ronaldo, The Mirror, *January 2009*

Q You're fast, you can dribble, and you score great goals. What makes you special?

A "I was born this way! But if you have quality and do not train every day you will go nowhere."

Cristiano Ronaldo, realmadridzone.com, 2010

During Ronaldo's six years in Manchester, he grew from a talented but often frustrating player into a guaranteed match winner. In the 2007–2008 season, he broke George Best's 40-year record for the most goals scored by a midfield player—42—in all competitions. Season after season he grew quicker, stronger, his free kicks more accurate, and he became so important to the team that Manchester United fans worried about how their team would cope without him!

In Spain, Ronaldo continued his goal scoring, with 26 goals in his first season. Madrid was beaten to the title by an amazing Barcelona team, but no one would bet against Ronaldo helping Real Madrid lift the Spanish title very soon.

Ronaldo plays for Portugal against the Czech Republic in Geneva, Switzerland, in 2008.

Steven Gerrard

LIVERPOOL'S SUPERMAN

Steven Gerrard in March 2010.

Stats!

Name: Steven George Gerrard

Date of birth: May 30, 1980

Clubs: Liverpool (1998–present)

Position: Center midfield

First break: Gerrard was spotted by Liverpool scouts at eight years old playing for his hometown team Whiston Juniors, in England. He joined Liverpool's youth academy at nine and signed his first professional contract in November 1997. Gerrard made his first team debut in November 1998 and played 13 times that season, often as a replacement for the team's injured captain, Jamie Redknapp.

Major achievements: Gerrard won the Champions League with Liverpool in 2005. He has also won two FA Cups (2001, 2006), two Football League Cups (2001, 2003), and a Union of European Football Associations (UEFA) Cup (2001).

Secrets of success: Steven Gerrard has all the skills a modern soccer player needs. He is fast, a great tackler, can pass the ball long or short, and can score not only spectacular but also important goals. His goals in the 2005 Champions League and 2006 FA Cup Finals took both games into extra time and helped Liverpool win the trophies.

Steven Gerrard's inspiration is his cousin Jon-Paul, who died in a 1989 stadium accident that killed 96 soccer fans.

Life Story

Steven Gerrard is the ultimate competitor. As someone who was born in Liverpool, England, and has played for one club his entire career, he is his team's main source of inspiration. He leads by example and never stops trying to bring success to Liverpool. He was named Man of the Match in Liverpool's Champions League final victory in 2005 and the FA Cup Final the following year.

Gerrard made his England team debut in 2000. He played in the 2000 and 2004 European Championships and the 2006 and 2010 World Cup tournaments. In South Africa, he was made England captain when Rio Ferdinand's knee injury forced him to miss the tournament. Gerrard was one of the team's most consistent performers and scored in the 1-1 draw with the United States team.

Questions and Answers

Q What's it like playing under a foreign manager?

A "I've worked with plenty of foreign coaches and it's been brilliant. Gerard Houllier and Rafa Benitez [for Liverpool], and [Sven-Goran] Eriksson and [Fabio] Capello for England. These are [soccer] people, they're winners. It doesn't matter what nationality they are. It's brought me on as a player and I feel like I've learned from their contrasting methods."

Steven Gerrard, fourfourtwo.com, 2008

Q What would it feel like to win the Premier League with Liverpool?

A "To win the title here, at Liverpool, would mean a lot more than winning seven or eight trophies at another club. Here, I can share it with my family, with the Liverpool supporters. I have always been one of them."

Steven Gerrard, The Mirror, June 2009

Gerrard has won several awards. He was named PFA Young Player of the Year in 2000 and PFA Player of the Year in 2006. He has been included in the PFA Team of the Year for the past six seasons. In 2007 he received an MBE (Master of the British Empire) from Queen Elizabeth II.

David Villa

SPANISH HITMAN

Barcelona's new signing, David Villa, at Camp Nou Stadium, in Barcelona, Spain, in May 2010.

Stats!

Name: David Villa Sánchez

Date of birth: December 3, 1981 in Tuilla, Asturias, Spain

Clubs: Sporting Gijón (1999–2003), Real Zaragoza (2003–2005), Valencia (2005–2010), Barcelona (2010–present)

Position: Striker

First break: Villa grew up in the northern Spanish region of Asturias. He tried out for one of the area's biggest teams, Real Oviedo, but was turned down because at 5 feet 9 inches (1.8 m) tall, he was thought to be too short. Luckily, he was accepted at another local club, Sporting Gijón. He worked his way through the youth ranks and made his first team debut in 2000.

Major achievements: Villa won the Copa del Rey (the equivalent of the FA Cup) with Real Zaragoza in 2004 and with Valencia in 2008. Most important, he is Spain's all-time top scorer and helped his country win Euro 2008 and the 2010 World Cup.

Secrets of success: Villa is naturally right-footed, but broke his right leg when he was a child. While his leg was in a cast, his father threw a soccer ball to him for hours, forcing him to kick with his left foot. He is now just as deadly with both feet!

Villa has his daughter Zaida's name embroidered on one of his soccer cleats and the Spanish flag on the other.

Life Story

David Villa is one of the world's best strikers. Until his move to Barcelona in the summer of 2010, he had never played for one of Europe's biggest clubs. His excellent ball control, clever movement, and deadly shooting accuracy have helped him score nearly 200 goals for some of Spain's smaller teams, though.

Questions and Answers

Q Who has been the biggest influence on your career?

A "My dad has always supported me and cheered me up until my career came around. I can barely remember a single training session when [he] wasn't there. I have never been alone on a [soccer field]."

David Villa, soccerlens.com, 2008

Q Who is your perfect strike partner?

A "Fernando Torres. We complement each other very well. We get on well on the [field] and very well off it too. We're a good partnership. We chase down defenders, put pressure on, and fight to create chances for each other. We work well together."

David Villa, The Scotsman, *June 2009*

Villa began his career in the Spanish Second Division, scoring an average of one goal every two games for Sporting Gijón. He kept up that average when he transferred to Real Zaragoza in the First Division, and then scored 101 goals in just 180 appearances when he joined Valencia.

He has enjoyed success with the Spanish national team too. Spain ended a 44-year wait for an international trophy by winning Euro 2008, and although Villa missed the final because of injury, he scored four goals in the four games he played, making him the tournament's top scorer. He is also Spain's top scorer in World Cup finals, with eight goals (three in 2006 and five in 2010). Defenders, beware of the Spanish hitman!

Villa in a Spanish League match between RCD Espanyol and Valencia in May 2010.

Carlos Tévez

BACKSTREET HERO

Tévez is revealed as the new Manchester City signing in July 2009.

When Tévez played for Corinthians, he was the first non-Brazilian to win their Player of the Year award in 30 years!

Stats!

Name: Carlos Alberto Tévez (born Carlos Alberto Martínez)

Date of birth: February 5, 1984

Clubs: Boca Juniors in Argentina (2001–2004), Corinthians in Brazil (2004–2006), West Ham United (2006–2007), Manchester United (2007–2009), Manchester City (2009–present)

Position: Striker

First break: Tévez was spotted playing soccer in the street and signed by his first club, All Boys, at just eight years old. At 13 he joined Boca Juniors' youth team, scoring 70 goals in four years.

Major achievements: He won the league with Boca Juniors (2002–2003) and Corinthians (2004–2005). He won the Premier League (2007–2008, 2008–2009) and Champions League (2008) with Manchester United. He also won a Gold medal with Argentina at the 2004 Olympics.

Secrets of success: Tévez grew up in one of the most dangerous neighborhoods in Buenos Aires, Argentina, known for its violence, drugs, and poverty. His father was often out of work, and his mother stayed at home to bring up Tévez and his four brothers and sisters.

Life Story

Carlos Tévez grew up in the slums of Ejército de los Andes, Aregentina, playing soccer on the streets to earn money to buy food. A born fighter, he brings the same determination and will to win to all the professional teams he has represented.

At 10 months old Tévez poured a kettle of boiling water over himself, causing third-degree burns and putting him in hospital for two months. The accident left him with a scar on the right side of his face, neck, and chest. However, he refused to have plastic surgery, as a series of operations would have stopped him from playing soccer for four months! He later refused an offer from his first professional team, Boca Juniors, to have the scars cosmetically improved, saying they were a part of "who he was in the past and who he is today."

Tévez, with Manchester City, plays against Liverpool in the FA Premier League, 2010.

Questions and Answers

Q Who are the best fans you have played in front of?

A "West Ham. Their supporters "feel" [soccer]. They are passionate. These people invested great support in me. I want to play for West Ham again before I finish my career. I have some unfinished business there."
Carlos Tévez, The Daily Mail, April 2010

Q Which sportsmen do you most admire?

A "Tiger Woods, Roger Federer, and Lionel Messi. They perform with excellence, like most of us could never dream of. These men create history with their level of performances. It is sport at another level. They are winning machines."
Carlos Tévez, The Daily Mail, April 2010

Tévez is a fierce competitor with an excellent scoring record. His goals saved West Ham United from being moved to a lower division in 2007, and he found the net 23 times in 35 appearances in his first season with Manchester City. Tévez plays to win.

Wesley Sneijder

DEAD BALL SPECIALIST

Sneijder lifts the UEFA Champions League trophy after the final against Bayern Munich, 2010.

Stats!

Name: Wesley Benjamin Sneijder

Date of birth: June 9, 1984

Clubs: Ajax in the Netherlands (2002–2007), Real Madrid in Spain (2007–2009), Inter Milan in Italy (2009–present)

Position: Midfield

First break: At seven years old, Sneijder joined Ajax's youth academy in Amsterdam, the Netherlands. Like Barcelona's La Masia, the Ajax academy is famous for producing some of the best soccer players in Europe. Sneijder made his first team debut for Ajax at 18.

Major achievements: He has won the Dutch league with Ajax (2003–2004) and the Spanish league with Real Madrid (2007–2008). In the 2009–2010 season he won the "treble" with Inter Milan—the Italian league, Italian Cup, and the UEFA Champions League.

Secrets of success: At 5 feet 7 inches (1.7 m) tall, Sneijder is relatively short, but he is fast and strong on the field. Like David Beckham, he is a "dead ball specialist." He has been the first-choice free kick taker for all the teams he has played for.

To help him practice with his weaker left foot, Ajax coaches blew a whistle and stopped training every time Sneijder touched the ball with his right foot!

Life Story

The 2009–2010 season put Wesley Sneijder on the map. The Dutch-born attacking midfielder won the domestic treble with Inter Milan and then helped the Netherlands to their third World Cup Final. Sneijder was the tournament's joint top scorer with five goals.

Sneijder spent the early part of his career with Ajax before a move to Real Madrid, in Spain. The big transfer fee made him the second most expensive Dutch player ever, behind Ruud van Nistelrooy. He

Questions and Answers

Q Which position do you most enjoy playing in?

A "I think I play best right behind the strikers, as an attacking midfielder. I like the coach to give me freedom, thanks to which I score many goals."

Wesley Sneijder, realmadridportal.com, August 2008

Q What made you leave the Netherlands and start playing abroad?

A "It's hard to explain. There comes a time in which a [soccer] player suddenly wants more. I'd played in the Dutch League for five years and I had a very good run, which gave me the chance of joining Real Madrid. You have to grab that chance and do things well in order to be able to say you made the right decision."

Wesley Sneijder, bbc.co.uk, 2008

Sneijder dribbles the ball past Russia's Konstantin Zyryanov in Euro 2008.

got off to a great start with a goal in his debut for Real Madrid, but unfortunately suffered a serious knee injury in his second season and struggled to regain his place in the team.

When Madrid sold Sneijder to Inter Milan for around half of what they had paid for him, everyone assumed his best performances were behind him. However, a glittering first season at Inter Milan and an eye-catching World Cup have made Snejider an international talent to watch.

David Beckham

GREAT BRITON

Beckham was the player liaison for England at the World Cup in 2010.

Beckham says if he didn't play soccer, he would like to build Lego sets for a living!

Stats!

Name: David Robert Joseph Beckham

Date of birth: May 2, 1975

Clubs: Manchester United (1993–2003), Real Madrid, in Spain (2003–2007), Los Angeles Galaxy (2007–present), on loan to AC Milan (2009 and 2010)

Position: Midfielder

First break: Beckham had youth trials with Tottenham Hotspur, Leyton Orient, and Norwich City, but signed with Manchester United on his 14th birthday. Alongside players such as Ryan Giggs and Paul Scholes, he won the FA Youth Cup in 1992 and made his first team debut in the same year.

Major achievements: With Manchester United he won the Premier League six times between 1995 and 2003, the FA Cup twice (1996 and 1999) and the UEFA Champions League (1999). He also won the Spanish League with Real Madrid (2006–2007).

Secrets of success: At his peak, Beckham was recognized as the best crosser of the ball and the best free kick taker in the world. Manchester United manager Alex Ferguson said he "practiced with a discipline to achieve an accuracy that other players wouldn't care about."

Life Story

David Beckham is one of the most talented, and certainly the most famous, soccer player that Britain has ever produced. Beckham left home at 14 to join his boyhood idols, Manchester United. He rose through the ranks alongside a talented generation of young players. In ten years with the first team he won every prize in the English game, including the Premier League, FA Cup, and Champions League.

In 2003, Beckham moved to Real Madrid, in Spain. He quickly became a favorite with the fans at the club because of his skills and hard work. In his final season in Spain, he helped Madrid win the Spanish league title.

Now playing for Los Angeles Galaxy, Beckham's worldwide popularity is helping to raise the profile of soccer in the United States where the sport has to compete with basketball, baseball, and football for the fans' attention.

Beckham with Los Angeles Galaxy in 2009.

Questions and Answers

Q What have you learned from the managers you've worked with?

A "I've been lucky to work with some of the greatest managers in [soccer.] Sir Alex Ferguson was like a father to me. He looked after me all the way up to the time I left [the club.] Fabio Capello is different tactically. He's Italian, they're best at that."
David Beckham, The Mirror, *July 2010*

Q How did you get so good at free kicks?

A "I go through situations the night before, sometimes I even lie awake at night thinking about [what to do.] When kids ask me what they have to do to become a professional, I tell them to practice. I'm 35 and I still practice!"
David Beckham, The Mirror, *July 2010*

Beckham married former Spice Girls singer Victoria Adams in 1999. The couple is never far from newspaper headlines. They have three sons named Brooklyn, Romeo, and Cruz, and a daughter named Harper.

Andrés Iniesta

PASS MASTER

Iniesta and the Spanish team received a heroes' welcome in Barcelona, Spain, after winning the World Cup in 2010.

Stats!

Name: Andrés Iniesta Luján

Date of birth: May 11, 1984

Clubs: Barcelona (2002–present)

Position: Midfield

First break: Iniesta was spotted by Barcelona scouts as a 12 year old playing for his local youth team. The club invited him to become part of their famous La Masia training academy, where fellow players Lionel Messi and Cesc Fabregas were also students. Iniesta had to leave home and move 310 miles (500 km) across the country to join.

Major achievements: He has won the Spanish league four times with Barcelona (2004–2005, 2005–2006, 2008–2009, 2009–2010) and the Champions League twice (2006, 2009). He has also won Euro 2008 and the 2010 World Cup with Spain.

Secrets of success: From as young as eight, Iniesta was determined to succeed. Twice a week he left school at lunchtime, traveled 45 minutes each way to practice with his youth team, and then came back to his school desk for his afternoon lessons. He was exhausted, but happy!

Iniesta's grandfather ran the village bar. The whole family worked there, except young Andrés. He was always too busy playing soccer!

Life Story

After Barcelona beat Manchester United 2–0 in the 2009 Champions League final, Wayne Rooney described Andrés Iniesta as the best player in the world. Playing in a Barcelona team alongside FIFA World Player of the Year Lionel Messi, that was quite an achievement!

Iniesta plays as an attacking midfielder for Barcelona and for Spain. He and fellow midfielder Xavi Hernández share an unspoken understanding of each other's games and together have conquered Europe and the world.

Questions and Answers

Q   What was it like moving so far away from your family at 12?

A   "The first few months were [hard]. I only saw my parents once or twice a month. I was lucky to have fantastic [friends] like [Carlos] Puyol and Victor Valdes. They helped me get used to my situation."

Andrés Iniesta, bbc.co.uk, 2010

Q   Why do you think Spain is currently so successful?

A   "[Fellow midfielder] Xavi and I have played together for years and sometimes you don't need to think or look to know where he will be or what he's going to do. But we have also benefitted from Cesc [Fabregas], [David] Villa, and so on. The style of all the players fits together so well."

Andrés Iniesta, fourfourtwo.com, June 2010

In fact, in a moment straight out of a kid's wildest fantasy, it was Iniesta who scored the goal in extra time that helped Spain win the 2010 World Cup.

The midfielder is willing and able to play anywhere on the field to help his team—from winger to central midfield to second striker. His abilities have prompted Barcelona to add a clause to his contract to scare off any clubs who might want to buy him!

Iniesta prepares to score the winning goal in the World Cup Final against the Netherlands in 2010.

Rio Ferdinand

WORLD-CLASS DEFENDER

The England captain Rio Ferdinand in May 2010.

Apart from playing soccer, Rio Ferdinand has launched an Internet magazine (www.rioferdinand.com) and produced a Hollywood movie!

Stats!

Name: Rio Gavin Ferdinand

Date of birth: November 7, 1978

Clubs: West Ham United (1995–2000), Leeds United (2000–2002), Manchester United (2002–present)

Position: Central defender

First break: Ferdinand joined West Ham's youth academy in 1992 after being spotted by Frank Lampard's father. Lampard was also a trainee at the academy.

Major achievements: He has won the Premier League with Manchester United four times (2002–2003, 2006–2007, 2007–2008, and 2008–2009.) They also won the Champions League in 2008, beating Chelsea in the final.

Secrets of success: Ferdinand grew up without much money in southeast London, England. However, the guidance and advice of his parents kept him away from gangs and violence. At 11 years old, he won a scholarship to the Central School of Ballet in London, traveling to classes four days a week for four years. The ballet training improved his balance and strength. Ferdinand was nicknamed "Pele" by his first youth coach for his composure with the ball.

Life Story

Rio Ferdinand is one of England's most talented defenders. A strong header of the ball, with excellent positional sense and a will-to-win attitude, he is often compared to Bobby Moore, England's 1966 World-Cup-winning captain. Ferdinand has played a big part in Manchester United's success.

The defender spent five years with West Ham United, alongside fellow England stars Frank Lampard and Joe Cole. When he joined Leeds United in 2000 he became Britain's most expensive defender. Then he joined Manchester United in 2002 and became the most expensive British soccer player in history!

Ferdinand, with Manchester United, plays in the FA Premier League in 2010.

Questions and Answers

Q Why do you think you succeeded as a soccer player?

A "I always wanted to be a professional [soccer player], and there was nothing really going to get in my way. I used to leave my [friends] and take trains and buses to West Ham. That was my whole life when I was growing up."

Rio Ferdinand, The Guardian, *March 2010*

Q What skills does it take to be a good captain?

A "There are different types of leaders. There's the guy who shouts and screams, and the guy who leads by example. I do a bit of both. I lead by example, but when somebody needs to be told, I never shirk that responsibility."

Rio Ferdinand, The Guardian, *March 2010*

Ferdinand has played over 80 times for England, making his debut in 1997 at 19 years old. He played well for his country in the 2002 and 2006 World Cups, but unfortunately a knee ligament injury kept him out of the 2010 World Cup in South Africa. In typical fashion, he was fighting for his place again as soon as he was able. Ferdinand hopes to captain his country at the 2012 European Championships.

OTHER SOCCER STARS

Lionel Messi

Career

Background: Messi and his family left Argentina for Spain when he was just 13. Soccer talent scouts had seen him playing for local team Newell's Old Boys and recommended him to Barcelona. The club paid for expensive growth hormone treatments to help the player reach his current height of 5 feet 7 inches (1.7 m).

Current club: FC Barcelona (Spain) 2003–present.

International team: Argentina 2005–present.

Career highs: Won six trophies with Barcelona during the 2008–2009 season, including the Spanish League and the Champions League. Was named FIFA World Player of the Year in 2009. Scored 45 goals (including 34 in the league) for Barcelona in the 2009–2010 season.

Special skills: One of the best dribblers in the world. Excellent ball control, powerful left-foot shot.

Web site: www.lionelmessi.com

Basic Information

Home: Born in Rosario, Argentina. Lives in Barcelona, Spain.

Birthday: June 24, 1987

Ryan Giggs

Career

Background: Was signed by Manchester United manager Alex Ferguson at 14 when he watched Giggs score a hat trick against a Manchester United Under-15 team. Made his professional debut in 1991 and has been on the team ever since. Holds the record for most Manchester United appearances.

Current club: Manchester United 1990–present.

International team: Wales 1991–2007.

Career highs: Giggs has won more medals than any other player in English soccer history. Currently holds 11 league title medals, two Champions League medals, and four FA Cup medals. Was voted PFA Player of the Year and BBC Sports Personality of the Year in 2009.

Special skills: Great speed in his youth. With age, he has moved into center midfield to maximize his great passing abilities.

Web site: www.ryangiggs.cc

Basic Information

Home: Born in Cardiff, Wales. Lives in Manchester, England.

Birthday: November 29, 1973

Thomas Müller

Career

Background: Müller joined Bayern Munich at ten years old and worked his way up through youth and reserve teams, making his professional debut in 2008. Signed his first senior contract in February 2009. Broke into the first team and the German national team during the 2009–2010 season.

Current club: Bayern Munich (Germany) 2008–present.

International team: Germany 2010–present.

Career highs: Won the German league and cup double with Bayern in 2010. Reached the semifinals of the 2010 World Cup, before losing 1–0 to Spain. Müller was named Best Young Player at the tournament and won the Golden Boot for top scorer.

Special skills: Müller is adaptable and can play as a winger, attacking midfielder, or striker. Quick and a regular goal scorer.

Basic Information

Home: Born in Weilheim, West Germany. Lives in Munich, Germany.

Birthday: September 13, 1989

Cesc Fàbregas

Career

Background: Fàbregas started as a trainee with his local club, Barcelona, but joined Arsenal as a 16 year old, becoming the Gunners' youngest player ever. Established himself as an Arsenal first team regular in the 2004–2005 season, and returned to Barcelona in 2011.

Current club: Barcelona 2011–present.

International team: Spain 2006–present.

Career highs: Won the 2005 FA Cup and the 2007 League Cup with Arsenal. He was voted PFA Young Player of the Year in 2008. Won both the 2008 European Championship and the 2010 World Cup with Spain.

Special skills: Fàbregas is a playmaker. He makes things happen for the team with his passing abilities and his eye for space and opportunities. He took most of Arsenal's free kicks, corners, and penalties.

Basic Information

Home: Born in Vilassar de Mar, Spain. Lives in London, England.
Birthday: May 4, 1987

Diego Forlán

Career

Background: Forlán was born into a family of soccer players. His father played for Uruguay in the 1966 and 1974 World Cup tournaments, and his grandfather played for Independiente in Argentina. Young Forlán also had four successful years at Independiente before joining Manchester United and then Villarreal and Atlético Madrid, in Spain.

Current club: Inter Milan 2011–present.

International team: Uruguay 2002–present.

Career highs: Won the Premier League with Manchester United in 2002–2003 and the UEFA Europa League with Atlético Madrid in 2009–2010. Was presented with the Golden Ball as the best player of the 2010 World Cup.

Special skills: Forlán is a prolific goal scorer who is strong in the air and comfortable shooting with either foot.

Web site: www.diegoforlan.com/

Basic Information

Home: Born in Montevideo, Uruguay. Lives in Madrid, Spain.
Birthday: May 19, 1979

Didier Drogba

Career

Background: Drogba made his debut at 18 for the French second division club Le Mans. He didn't sign a professional contract until he was 21. Drogba played for Guincamp and Olympique de Marseille in the French first division before moving to Chelsea, in England.

Current club: Chelsea 2004–present.

International team: Ivory Coast 2002–present.

Career highs: Won the Premier League three times (2004–2005, 2005–2006, and 2009–2010) and the FA Cup three times (2007, 2009, 2010) with Chelsea. Was the Premier League's top scorer in 2007 and 2010. Voted African Footballer [soccer player] of the Year in 2006 and 2009.

Special skills: Drogba is very strong with a powerful and accurate shot. He is a great finisher. When he gets a chance to score, he rarely misses!

Web site: www.didierdrogba.com/en/

Basic Information

Home: Born in Abidjan, Ivory Coast. Lives in London, England.
Birthday: March 11, 1978

Glossary

competition *(kom-pih-TIH-shun)* A game or test.
contract *(KAHN-trakt)* An official agreement between two or more people.
debut *(DAY-byoo)* A first public appearance, as of a performer or an athelete.
enthusiasm *(in–THOO-zee-ah-sum)* Happiness and willingness to do something.
league *(LEEG)* A group of sports teams.
match *(MACH)* A contest between two or more people or teams.
season *(SEE-zun)* The group of games for a year.
tournament *(TOR-nuh-ment)* A contest to see who wins the most games.

Index

Web Sites

Due to the changing nature of Internet links, PowerKids Press has developed an online list of Web sites related to the subject of this book. This site is updated regularly. Please use this link to access the list:
www.powerkidslinks.com/celeb/soccer/